T0059603

For Aaliyah, Arianna, Ava, Baaba, Charley, Chloe, C
Elijah, James, Jasper, Jean-Luc, Jojo, Joshua, Kaleb, Karson,
Kristian, Kurtis, Latoyah, Naima, Papa Prah, Ruby, Sha
Theodore, Tia, Tiann, Tinashe, Zachary, and the ones to co
—NEBH

To my little sister Vicky
—DM

THIS IS A BORZOI BOOK PUBLISHED BY ALFRED A. KNOPF

Text copyright © 2022 by Nana Ekua Brew-Hammond
Jacket art and interior illustrations copyright © 2022 by Daniel Minter

All rights reserved. Published in the United States by Alfred A. Knopf, an imprint of
Random House Children's Books, a division of Penguin Random House LLC, New York.

Knopf, Borzoi Books, and the colophon are registered trademarks of Penguin Random House LLC.

Visit us on the Web! rhcbooks.com

Educators and librarians, for a variety of teaching tools, visit us at RHTeachersLibrarians.com

Library of Congress Cataloging-in-Publication Data is available upon request.
ISBN 978-1-9848-9436-6 (trade) — ISBN 978-1-9848-9437-3 (lib. bdg.) — ISBN 978-1-9848-9438-0 (ebook)

The text of this book is set in 15-point Bodoni Egyptian Pro.
The illustrations were created using layers of acrylic wash on heavy watercolor paper.
Book design by Elizabeth Tardiff

MANUFACTURED IN CHINA
February 2022
10 9 8 7 6

First Edition

BLUE

A HISTORY OF THE COLOR AS DEEP
AS THE SEA AND AS WIDE AS THE SKY

By Nana Ekua Brew-Hammond

Illustrated by Daniel Minter

Alfred A. Knopf

New York

The color blue is all around us.
Have you ever wondered where it comes from?

It's in the sky, but you can't touch it.
It's in the sea, but when you cup it,
it disappears.

You can crush iris petals for a brilliant shade,
but just add water, and away
it fades.

But then blue appears in the strangest places,
discovered throughout history
in unexpected ways.

As early as 4500 BC,
diggers found blue rocks called lapis lazuli
in mines deep below Afghanistan's Sar-e-Sang valley.

Ancient Egyptians used
the rocks mostly to
make jewelry.
Some wore them as
charms, believing
they had the power
to protect people
from evil.
But with time, they
found new ways to use
this underground find.

By 44 BC, many Egyptians, including Queen Cleopatra VII,
were applying a bluish mixture around their eyes that looked
like eye shadow, made with ground lapis lazuli grains,
plants, and animal fat.

More than 600 years later,
artists began painting sculptures, walls, and canvases with
blue from the crushed rocks, too.

It was a royal pain for those who made the paint,
and so expensive, only the wealthy could buy it.

Since it was a luxury and in such high demand,
for centuries, scientists, merchants, and dyers looked for more sources of blue.

Then, on the shores of the
Mediterranean, Central America,
Mexico, and Japan,
dyers found blue in the belly of
certain shellfish.

A Phoenician myth says a dog discovered the color.
Finding a snail on the beach, the pup ate it up.

The snail turned the dog's tongue purple-blue,
and from that moment, a new industry was born.

Dyers had different ways of releasing the color.

In Mexico, they pressed the snail's foot.
In the Middle East, they cracked its shell.

Then they waited for the blue to appear.

Depending on the snail, the color starts out a milky white
or brownish yellow,
but once it's in the air and the sun,
it quickly turns green,
then reddish purple,
and with more sunlight,
blue.

But whether dyers pressed or cracked,
snail-blue was hard to produce.

Each snail released just one or two drops.
Imagine how many snails (and drops) it took to dye a royal robe,
not to mention enough fabric to fill a merchant's shop.

Perhaps because blue was
the color of the heavens,
yet so rare and hard to create
on earth,
people around the world
considered the color holy.

In an old Liberian folktale,
blue is explained as a gift
that connects God to humans.

In Italy, from the thirteenth
century onward, some artists began
reserving blue to paint the robes of
Mary, the mother of Jesus.

In Indonesia, some say
special prayers
to ward off evil spirits
before they make the dye.

In Israel, blue drapes hung in the temple
King Solomon built.
And many Jews still wear blue-d
threads called *tekhelet*.

For years, snail-blue was the most popular color,
but all along, there was another way to find blue in nature.

In parts of Asia, Africa, the Caribbean, and the Americas,
a group of plants in the pea family grew. They were called *Indigofera*.

There were a few different ways to get blue from these plants'
green leaves.
Indian dyers soaked them in water, while West African dyers
crushed and dried them.

When they added ashes or urin[...]
it enabled the dye to dissolve in [...] to fabric.

Since it was cheaper for dyers to produce blue from the indigo plant
than from rocks and snails,
and the shade was just as vibrant and long-lasting,
indigo dye—

especially indigo from India and
West Africa—was eventually valued
by most lovers of the color as
the best of the blues.
India and Nigeria became powerful centers
for making and trading indigo.

People made clothing, makeup, and medicine with it.

Indigo became so precious, people spent it like money.

In parts of Africa, some merchants
used strips of indigo cloth to buy people,
and sell them into slavery.

In India and Bangladesh, some planters
tricked or forced poor farmers
to grow indigo plants instead of food.

In the United States, some made
the African captives they had enslaved
farm indigo, calling the plant a cash crop
because it brought in a lot of money.

In this evil side of the trade for blue,
leaders and landowners around the world abused or
enslaved countless people just so
they could grow more indigo.

From the time blue was found,
scientists worked hard
to make a blue that wasn't so
difficult or cruel to produce.

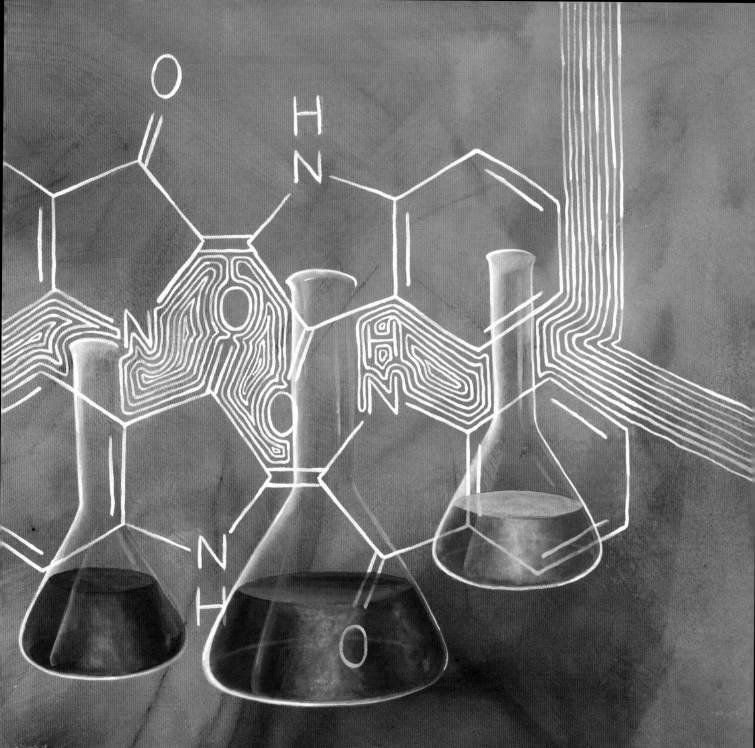

In 1865, scientist Adolf von Baeyer began trying,
and forty years later, in 1905, he won the Nobel Prize
for creating a chemical blue.

Finally, everyone—not just the wealthy—
could afford something blue.
But it was always about more than having a blue
outfit, piece of jewelry, or work of art.

Because of its scarcity, mystery,
and holy associations,
blue was more than a color.
It was a feeling.

We feel "blue" when we're sad,
perhaps because the people who had to dig,
grind, and grow
passed down their painful memories of
working the mines
or of slavery on indigo plantations.

Africans enslaved in America sang prayers
that sounded like tears.
The songs were called spirituals,
and they inspired a style of music called the blues,
originally known for its aching words and melodies.

We feel excited when something happens "out of the blue,"
perhaps because the color was once so rare—
a discovery that seemed to appear out of thin air.

And blue is still considered extraordinary,
as it was once the color of royalty.
This could be why, around the world,
blue ribbons are pinned for first prize.

Science Fair
Project
Solar Energy
Kit

Today, dyers still use indigo
to make blankets and clothing.

And some doctors still use it
as a natural medicine.

ecause blue has such a com   ed
   ry
of pain,
wealth,
invention,
and
recovery,

it's become a symbol of possibility,
as vast and deep as the bluest sea,
and as wide open and high
as the bluest sky.

Blue has so rich a history, it is more than a color. It is an expression of pleasant surprise and hope—why we say "out of the blue" or "nothing but blue skies"—and it is synonymous with feelings of sadness that comes with the style of music named after it. It signifies lasting loyalty ("true-blue"). It is associated with the wealthy ("royal blue"), yet everyone wears blue jeans. It refers to events that are incredibly rare, for example, "once in a blue moon," or things that are so big they can't be contained or controlled, like "the wild blue yonder."

The color itself has meant so many things to different cultures in history. In ancient texts from Asia to Europe, *blue* referred to a range of shades from sky blue to navy, turquoise to purple. Both *blue* and *purple* were used as catchall terms for this broad spectrum. Ancient Greeks explained blue in terms of how light or dark it was, likening it to white or gray or black or purple, but they didn't have a word for *blue*.

The physicist Sir Isaac Newton is credited with explaining how we see colors. The light we see every day is "split" into the colors that make it up—red, orange, yellow, green, blue, indigo, and violet. Newton's experiments, and those of scientists who came after him, showed that when you filter red out, you see blue. Water absorbs red naturally when there is lots of it; that's why the ocean looks blue until you cup it.

We also see blue differently depending on whether we're looking at the sky, the sea, or a physical object. Every color that hits our eyes is really just a short or long wave of light with high or low energy. Red is long and low-energy, while blue is short and high-energy. In the daylight, air scatters the light particles into short and fast waves, so the sky appears blue to us on a clear day.

What has never been in question is the desire for a rich and lasting blue. In ancient Egypt, and by the first century across Europe, dyers were producing a blue called woad from the *Isatis tinctoria* plant, but it was considered inferior to the blue dye generated from lapis lazuli or the indigo plant because woad faded.

Is it any wonder this mysterious hue was considered a holy gift from the gods by so many cultures? I was reading a description of King Solomon's temple in the Bible when the color blue seemed to jump out at me. *Why did it matter that one of the veils in the temple was blue?* I wondered, so I started researching the significance of the color. Much of what I learned is in this book.

WANT TO EXPLORE MORE?

A FEW BLUE FACTS

- Bamiyan, Afghanistan, is where the first known use of paint made from lapis lazuli was found, on two giant Buddha statues.

- Lapis lazuli is a gem made mostly of a complex salt mineral called lazurite, which ranges in color from deep blue to purple to blue-green. Found in Afghanistan, Chile, Siberia, northern Myanmar, Baffin Island in Canada, and the western part of the United States, it was historically used to make jewelry, as a mixture worn around the eyes to avoid infection and to offer divine protection, and as a rich blue paint.

- Cobalt was a source of blue found in mines in Persia (present-day Iran), used from the 1500s to beautify Persian mosques and tombs, as well as some of the precious ceramics and porcelain made in China during the Ming Dynasty.

- In 1704, the Swiss paint maker Herr Diesbach accidentally created a shade called Prussian blue, but it tended to turn gray over time.

- India has a historic tradition of developing special dyeing techniques. "Indigo," which means "Indian" or "blue dye from India," is believed to have gotten its name from European sailors, who brought it from India.

- Liberia was officially named in 1824 by Africans freed from slavery in America, but had been inhabited by Africans long before then. The country's name was taken from the Latin word *liber*, which means "free." A Liberian folktale says, in part, that water spirits appeared in a dream to a grieving mother named Asi to let her know that the salt of her tears, ashes, river water, urine, and wild indigo leaves were the secret ingredients that made the heavenly color.

- Nigeria was once a powerful center of indigo production, with dye pits in Kano, Nigeria, known to date back as far as 1498. Adire is a traditional Nigerian indigo fabric made by artisans who, traditionally, were always women. One style called adire eleko is made by painting cassava flour paste onto the cloth, then soaking it with dye for a designated time. In the final step, artisans thoroughly wash the cloth. The parts where the cassava flour was applied resist the dye, creating a stunning pattern.

- Phoenicia is an ancient territory on the seacoast of the Middle East that is believed to have encompassed present-day Lebanon, plus parts of Syria and Israel. During the twelfth century BC, Phoenicians were known around the world as sailors, fishermen, and traders. Also known for dyeing cloth with the purple dye they obtained from the *Murex trunculus* snail, their name became synonymous with the color. *Phoenicia* comes from the Greek word for "blood-red."

- South Carolina was an important part of the global indigo economy in the mid-1700s. When Eliza Lucas, then the sixteen-year-old daughter of a plantation owner, was given indigo seeds as a gift, she directed the people enslaved on her plantation who were skilled in growing and producing indigo dye to plant it. For a time, until the Revolutionary War began in 1775, indigo was more profitable than rice to the American economy.

- Tekhelet is a blue made from the secretions of sea snails, which ranges in shade from turquoise to purple. It was highly valued and sacred in the ancient world, particularly in the Middle East. Part of the Jewish High Priest's uniform was blue, as were some veils in the temple King Solomon built and the tassels Jewish people were instructed to wear.

SELECTED SOURCES

"Adire—Indigo Resist Dyed Cloth from Yorubaland, Nigeria." Victoria and Albert Museum. Accessed April 30, 2020. vam.ac.uk/content/articles/a/adire-indigo-resist-dyed-cloth-from-yorubaland-nigeria/.

"Adolf von Baeyer, Biographical." NobelPrize.org. Accessed December 11, 2018. nobelprize.org/prizes/chemistry/1905/baeyer/biographical/.

Angier, Natalie. "Blue Through the Centuries: Sacred and Sought After." *New York Times.* October 22, 2012. nytimes.com/2012/10/23/science/blue-through-the-centuries-sacred-and-sought-after.html.

Anna, Cara. "Indigo, Ash and Time Mark Nigeria's Centuries-Old Dye Pits." Associated Press. February 21, 2019. apnews.com/899524e016af4d4ab81f3f07d306c70c.

Asiaticus. "The Rise and Fall of the Indigo Industry in India." *The Economic Journal.* June 1912. Vol. 22, No. 86. 237–247. jstor.org/stable/2221777.

Becker, Jill. "Cassava Resist Dyeing: Traditional Dyeing Techniques in a New Environment." Uwispace.sta.uwi.edu. Accessed April 30, 2020. uwispace.sta.uwi.edu/dspace/bitstream/handle/2139/15884/Cassava%20Resist%20Dyeing%20Becker.pdf?sequence=1.

The Bible. English Standard Version. Exodus 36:35, Numbers 15:38, 2 Chronicles 3:14. Available online at bible.com.

"Blue Light and Your Eyes." PreventBlindness.org. Accessed December 11, 2018. preventblindness.org/blue-light-and-your-eyes.

Bojer, Thomas Stege. "The History of Indigo Dyeing and How It Changed the World." Medium.com. June 9, 2017. Accessed April 30, 2020. medium.com/@tsbojer/the-history-of-indigo-dyeing-and-how-it-changed-the-world-35c8bc66f0e9.

Chakrabarti, Chitta Ranjan. "The Political Ideas of Sisir Kumar Ghosh." shodhganga.inflibnet.ac.in/bitstream/10603/165239/5/05_chapter%203.pdf.

Etymonline.com. etymonline.com/word/indigo.

Finlay, Victoria. *Color: A Natural History of the Palette.* New York: Random House Trade Paperbacks, 2004.

"Growing Indigo in South Carolina." Ancestry.com. Accessed December 11, 2018. ancestry.com/contextux/historicalinsights/indigo-south-carolina.

McKinley, Catherine E. *Indigo: In Search of the Color That Seduced the World.* New York: Bloomsbury USA, 2011.

Morris, Roderick Conway. "Lapis Lazuli and the History of 'the Most Perfect' Color." *New York Times.* August 18, 2015. nytimes.com/2015/08/19/arts/international/lapis-lazuli-and-the-history-of-the-most-perfect-color.html.

"The Nobel Prize in Chemistry, 1905." NobelPrize.org. Accessed September 19, 2018. nobelprize.org/prizes/chemistry/1905/summary/.

Prasad, Rajendra. "Indigo—The Crop That Created History and Then Itself Became History." Accessed April 30, 2020. insa.nic.in/writereaddata/UpLoadedFiles/IJHS/Vol53_3_2018__Art05.pdf.

Richardson, David, and Sue Richardson. Asian Textile Studies, "Indigo." Accessed December 11, 2018. asiantextilestudies.com/indigo.html.

Sterman, Baruch, and Judy Taubes. *The Rarest Blue: The Remarkable Story of an Ancient Color Lost to History and Rediscovered.* Guilford, Connecticut: Globe Pequot Press, 2012.

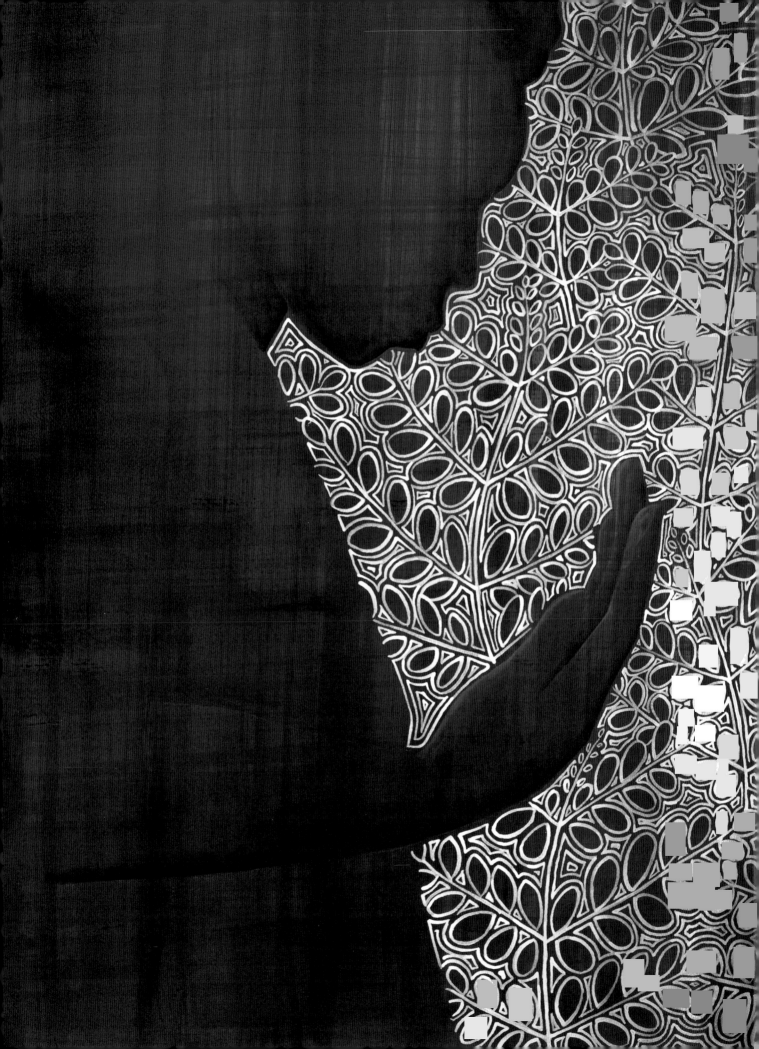